Unfolding the Basket: Book 1
Tabin Brooks

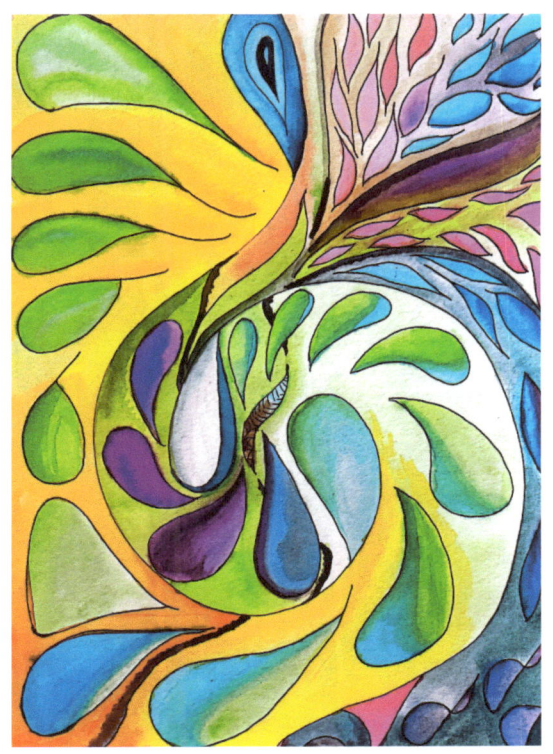

A selection of artwork and poetry for healing

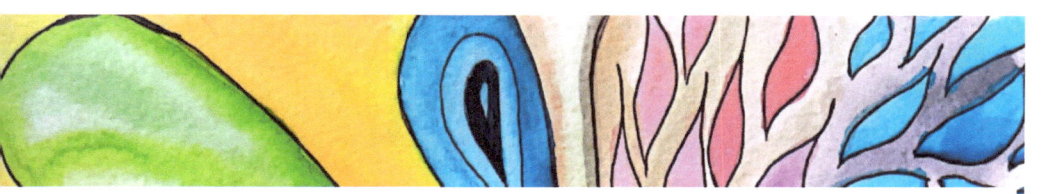

**Follower, unfold, for God
is good in change**

pain to paper
paper to poem
an alchemist's work
to physician, heal thyself

princess to pauper
pauper to power
to heal, to revive
to see the pathway to life

visions to dreamers
dreamers to futures
The untold unfolds
a process to bare a soul

basket to baloney
baloney to truth
the way of the word
to refold a basket of truth.

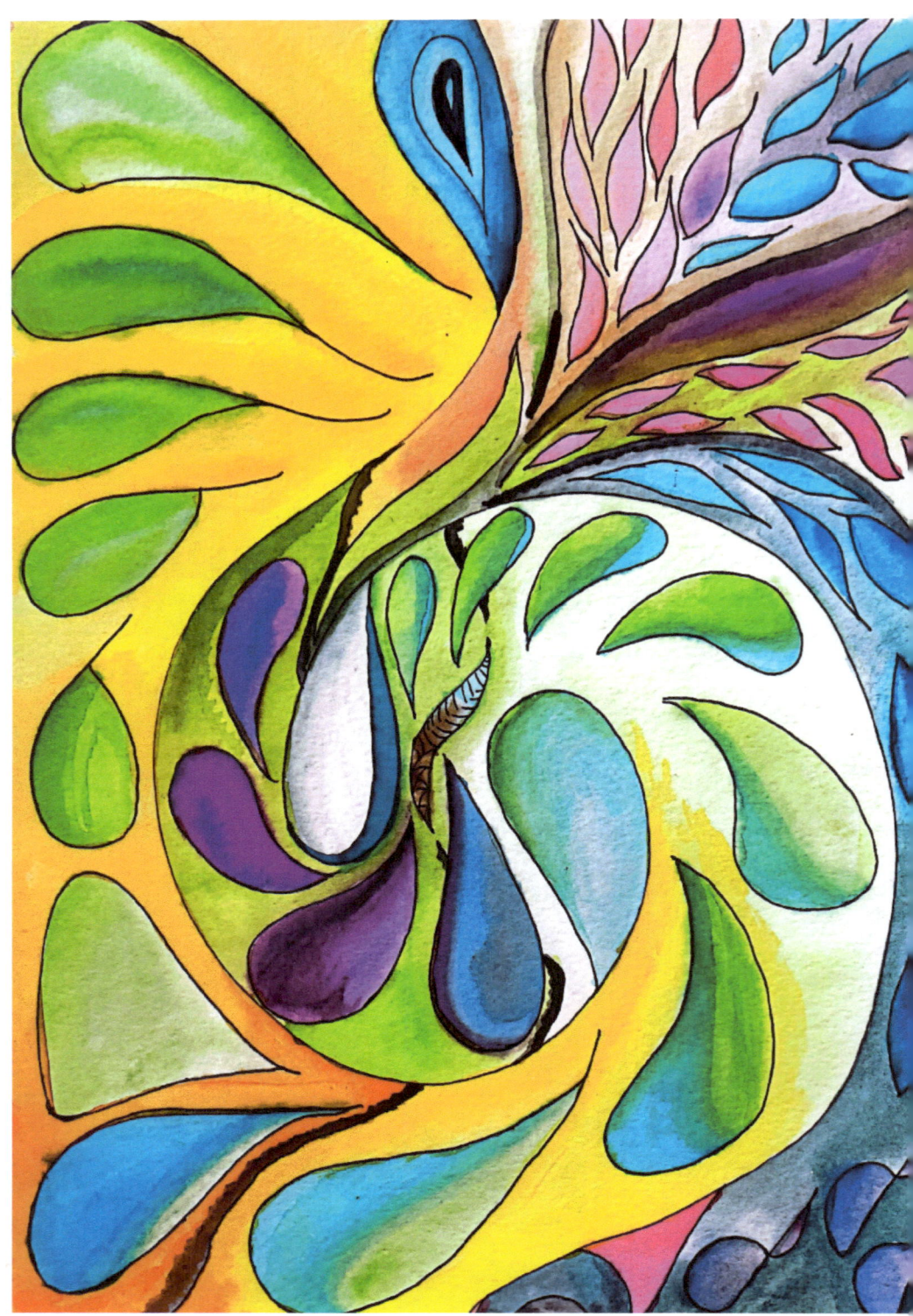

The creation of a soul

Memories swirl
Ancestors play games

Uno, chess and snap!
A grin, a win, a sin?

Perhaps – it's your turn
To roll the dice

A statistical miracle
A recombinate future

So, is that you?
Look at you, aren't you cute?

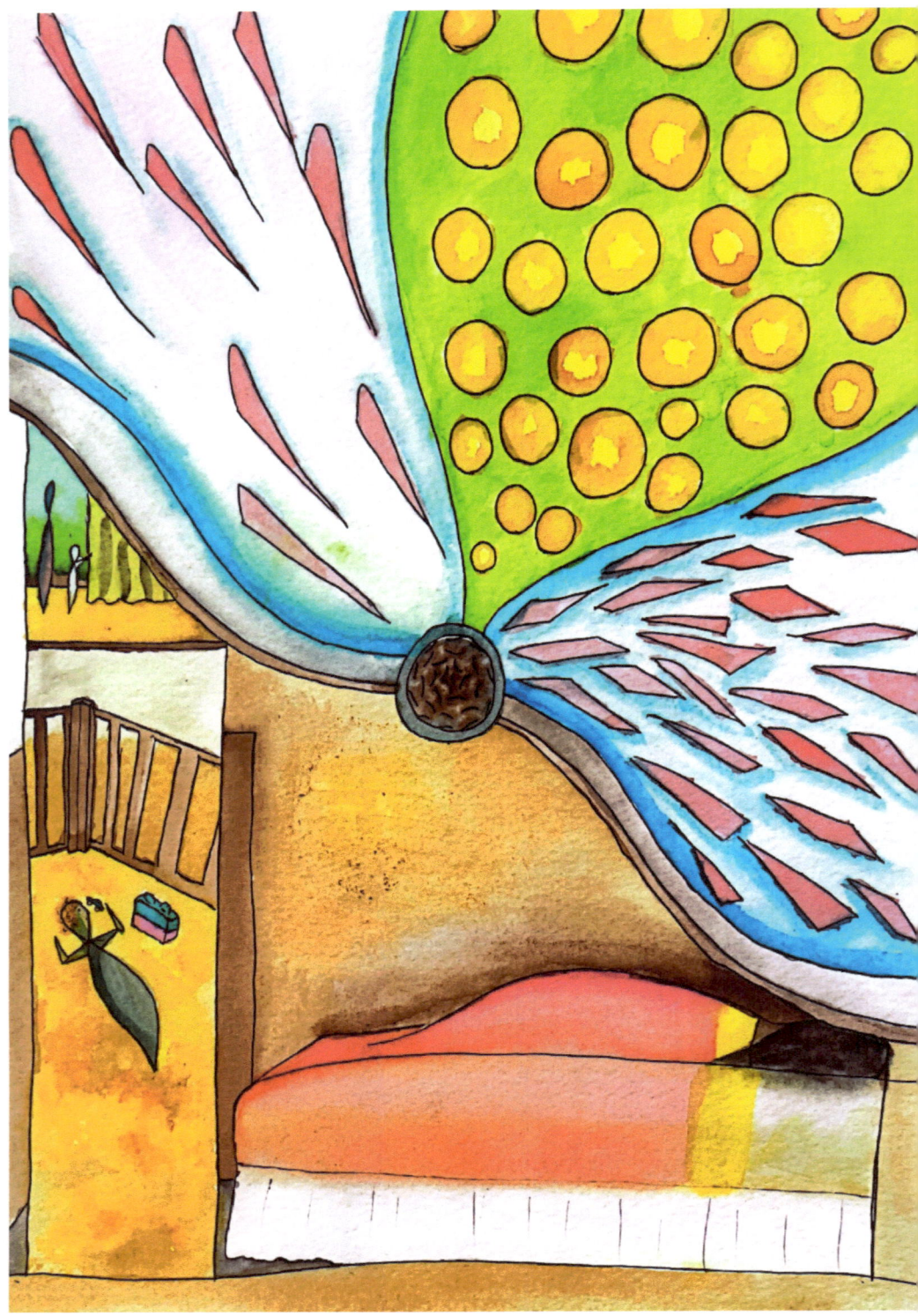

Separation!

Tragedy, loss
why, why, *why?*

Are they ever coming back?
Help me feel

My parents, they have gone
they have gone
they have gone away

Resignation, perhaps dramatic
Perhaps the book never reopens
A tragedy

(But look, the book is unclosed)

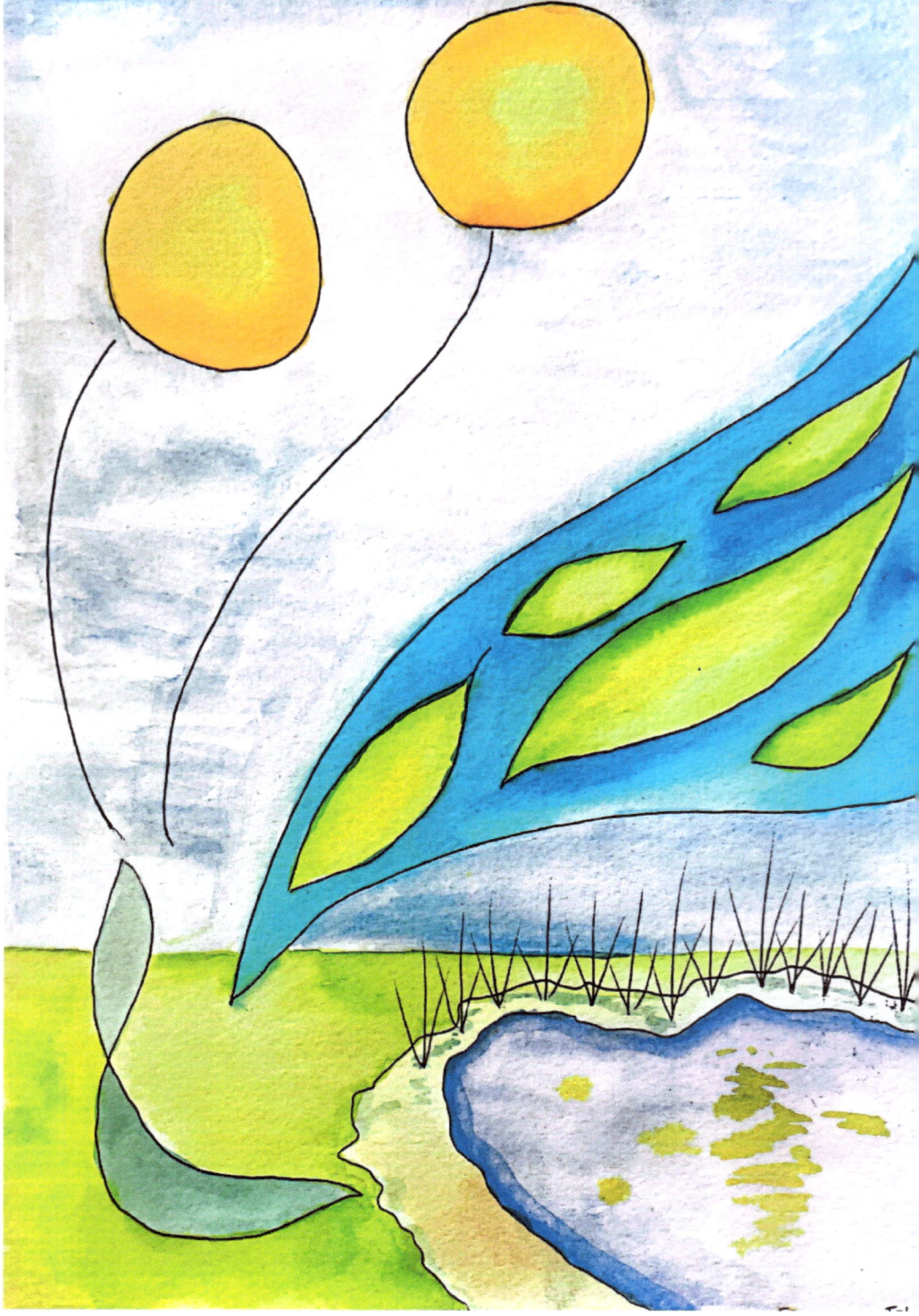

Mary, Mary

Sarah, Mary
Quite contrary
How does your garden grow?

Later I believe
because of this seed
and pretty fairies all in a row

Tabin, Mary
No longer contrary
For I have seen my garden grow

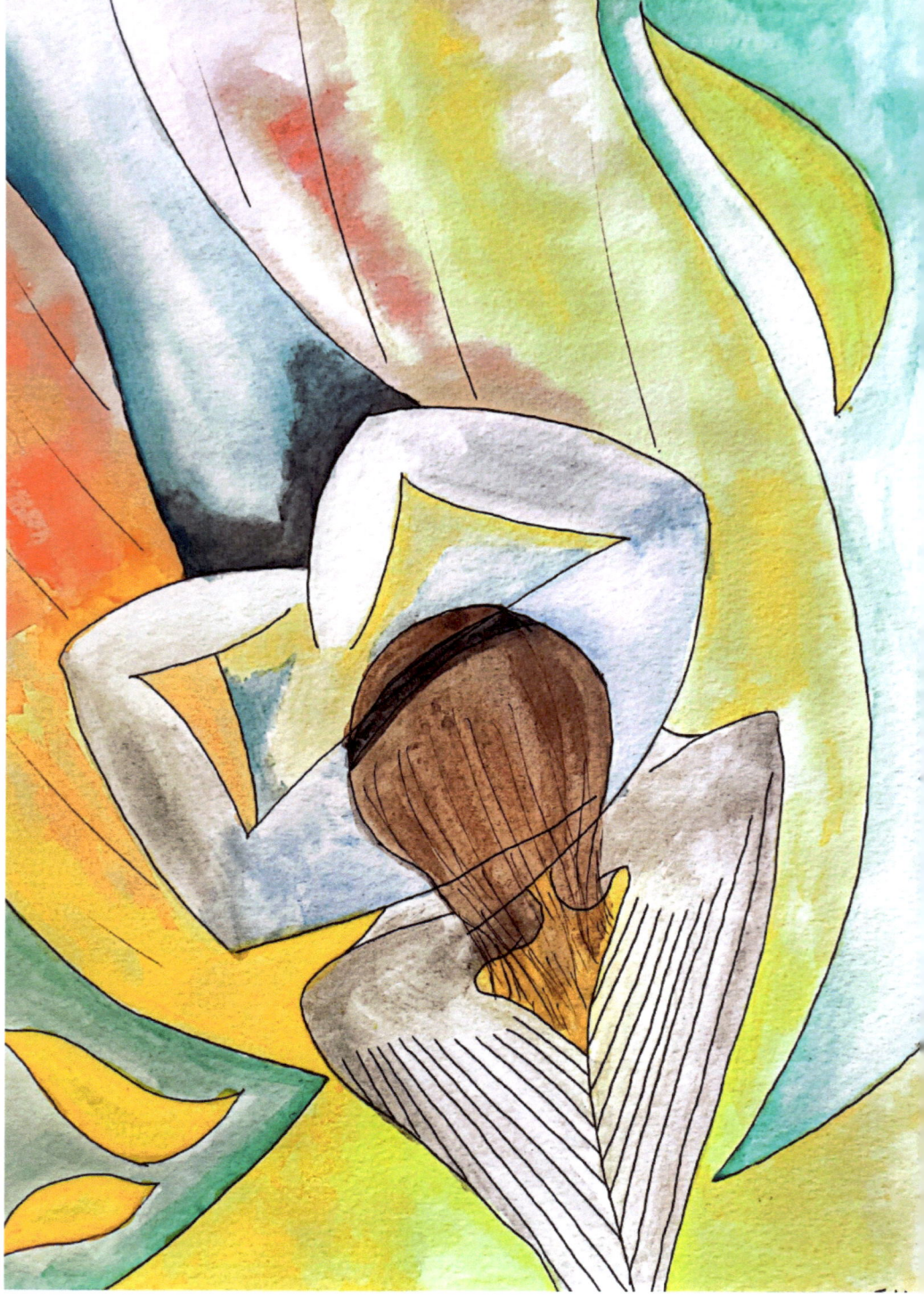

Atishu

Aitishu, Aitishu
we all fall down
A dramatic exit
Or all for show

Angel fallen
devastation felt in town
but life is good
make not too many changes

Of the fall itself
was there ever a need?
Or was it all in our heads
germinated,
sown,
risen...
cut for seed.

A cry, a plea
Let this fall stop with me.

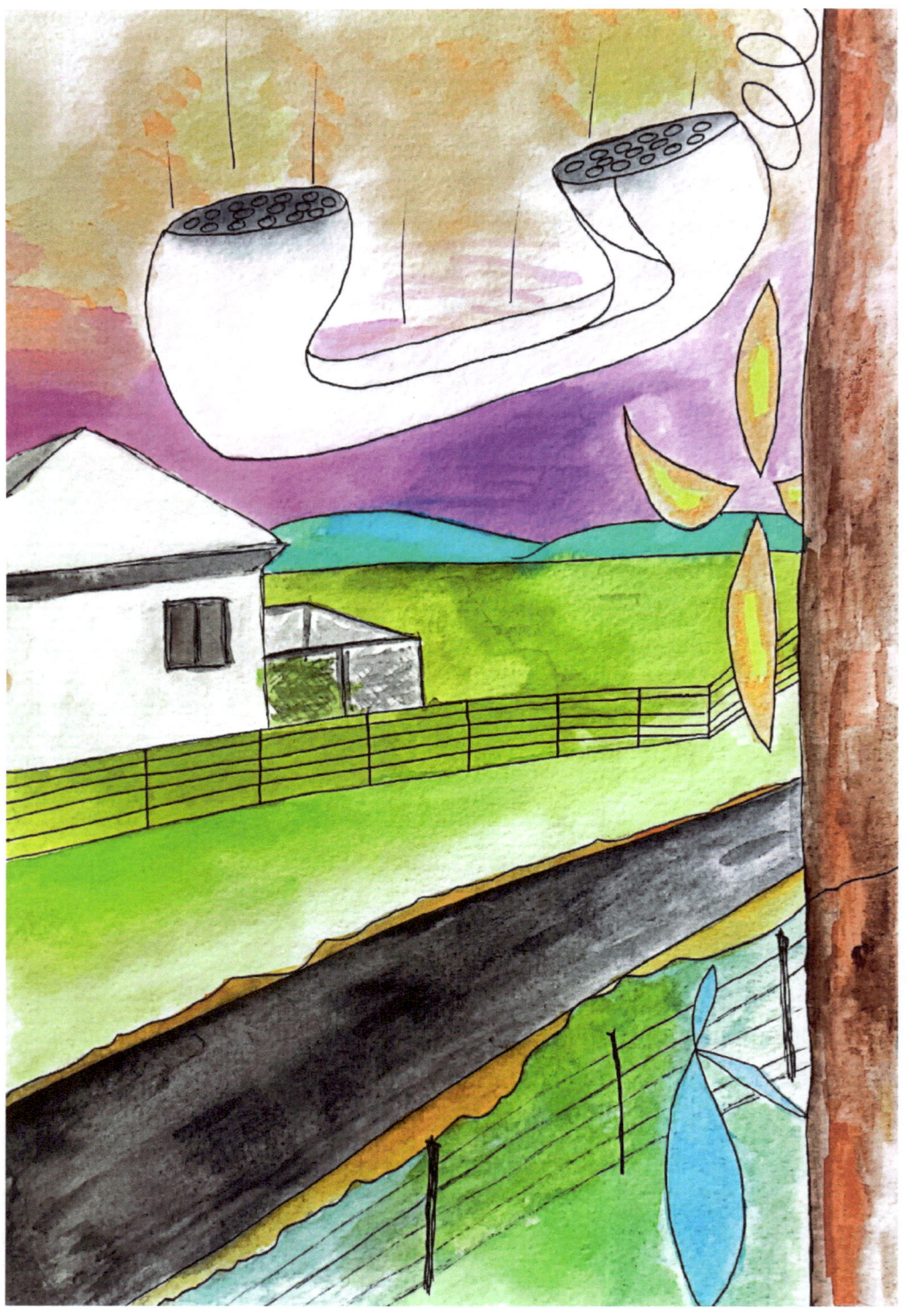

Call Undropped

A moment of understanding
To get out and wait
Wait for the call,
the sign
the way.

Wilful against a will of return
And so the long walk begins
At the end home
no matter the path

Moss underfoot, gravel reminds
that you left without shoes
Sirens appear
To carry you home

Connection made,
isolation no longer truth
Call answered and the path
walked, smoothed though

unrealised

until much later to
pick up the call, for God
answers prayer,
even that of the runaways
from reasons
and reason

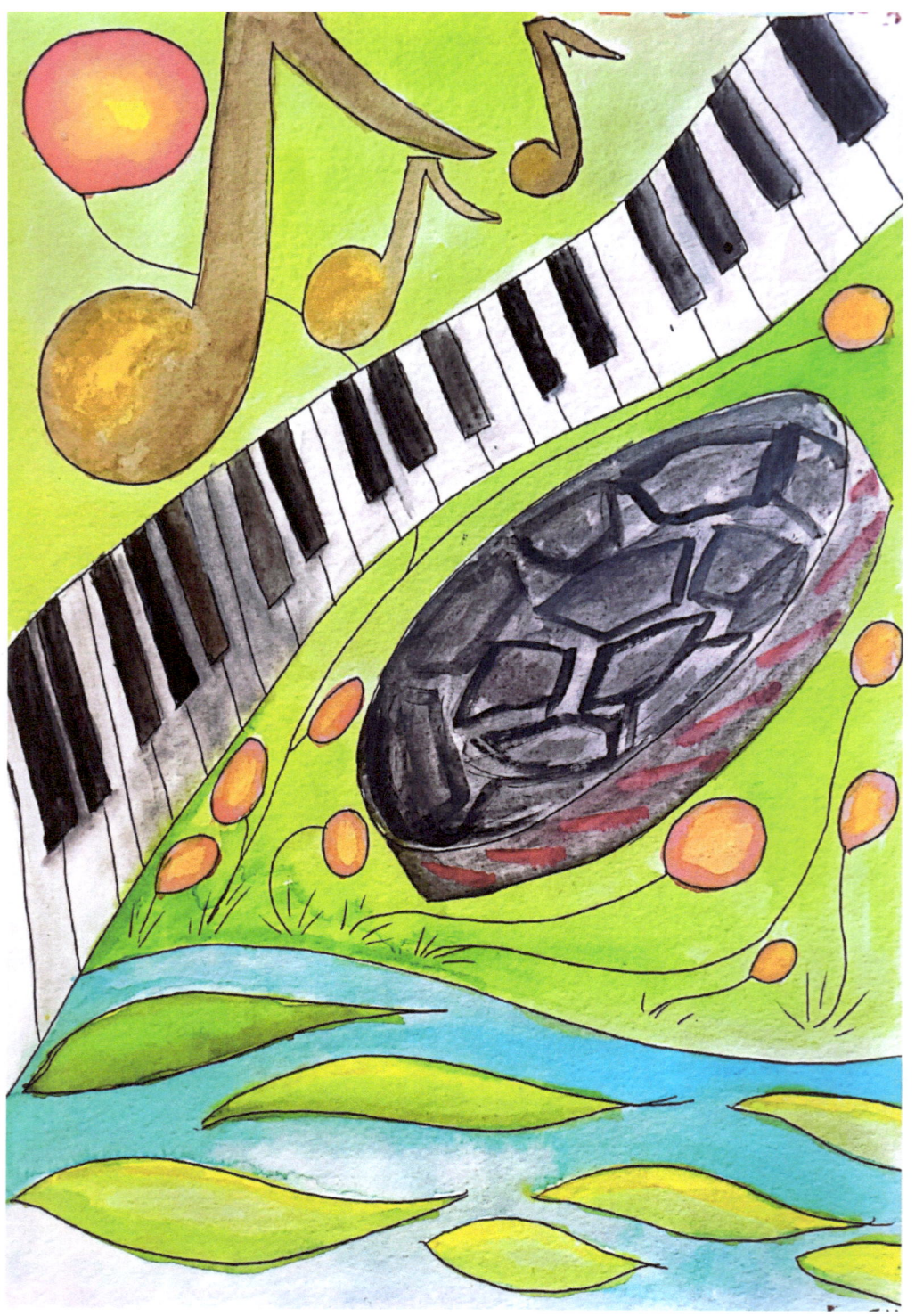

The Sound of Music

The beat of drum
not always a thud

The tune of keys
open to reveal strings

The river flowing
to it's tune of spirit

Connections made
in couplet of song

To heal the mind
and redeem the wrong

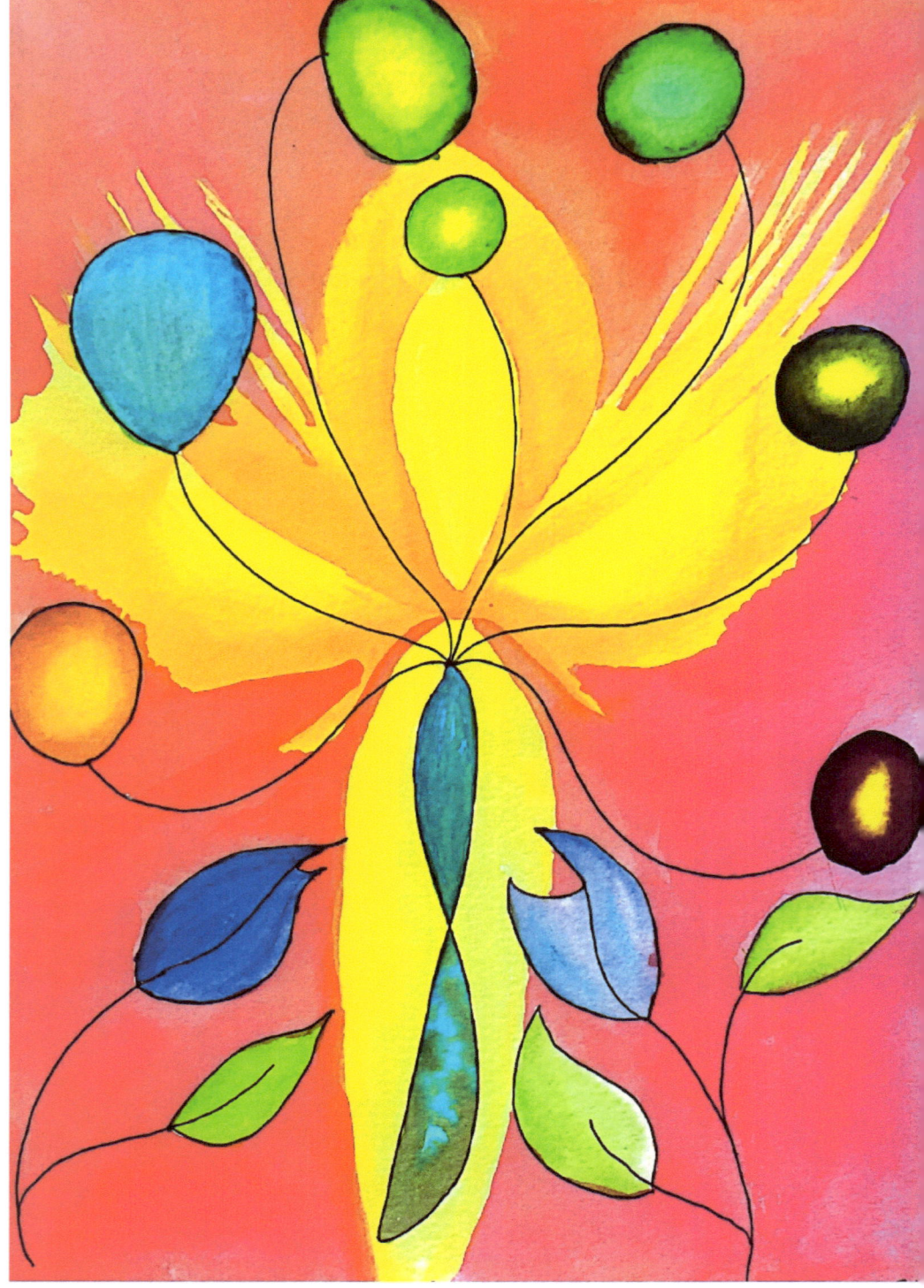

Ascension, Connected

Visions
Signs from a child
and a place
where it all makes
Sense

One and seven makes eight
God is our friend –
a good Aussie mate

Comfort in pain
coincidence manifest
we flourish
and rise to our
Best

Eight to infinity
Nine for change
Ten to build out of our cage

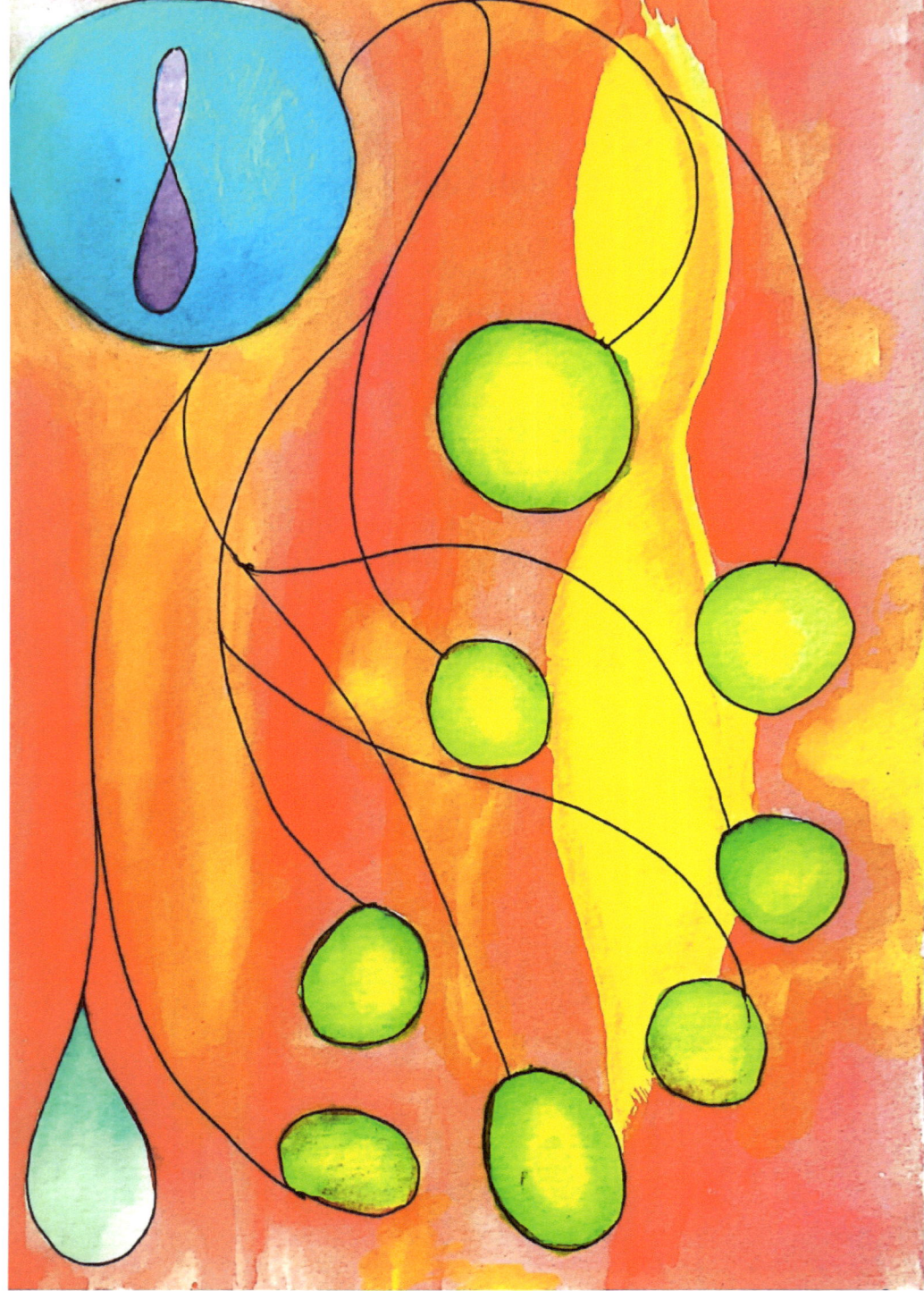

Connections

The friends we make
don't always stay
but those we know
are true stay firm

If forever be impossible
At least bring forth today

We connect, we change
We build, we grow
Together, then alone
Many arrows in one bow

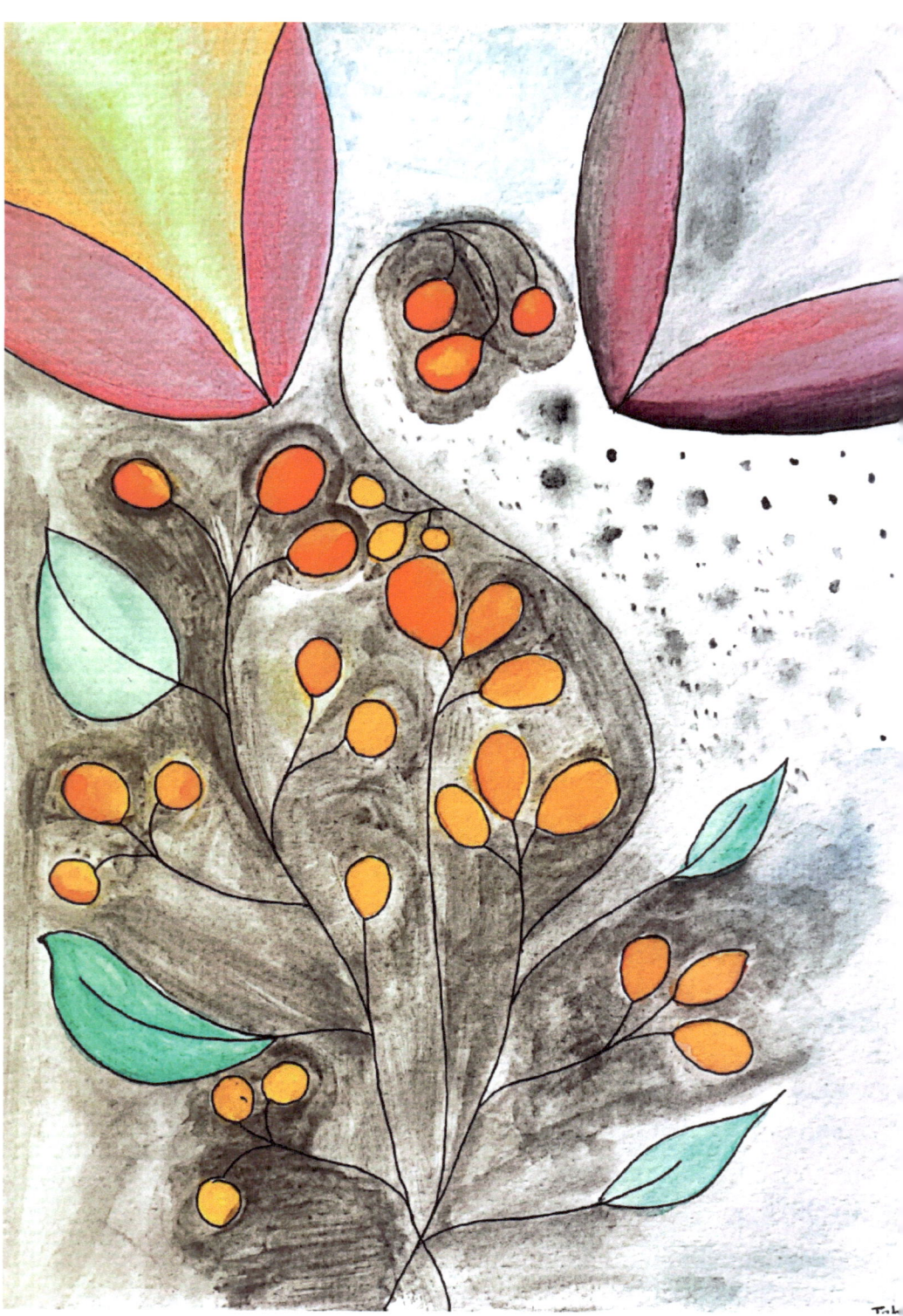

Golden Sun

Sun like showers
streaks of light
through the clouds

It's in my head
the fog. I miss
and mist.

The sun pours in
I open my eyes
to feel a better way

Connections made
lightbulb luminate
and tendrils emerge

From barren soil
comes new life
peeking through the fog

Gaining from positive
Shrinking from negative
All's left to do is live

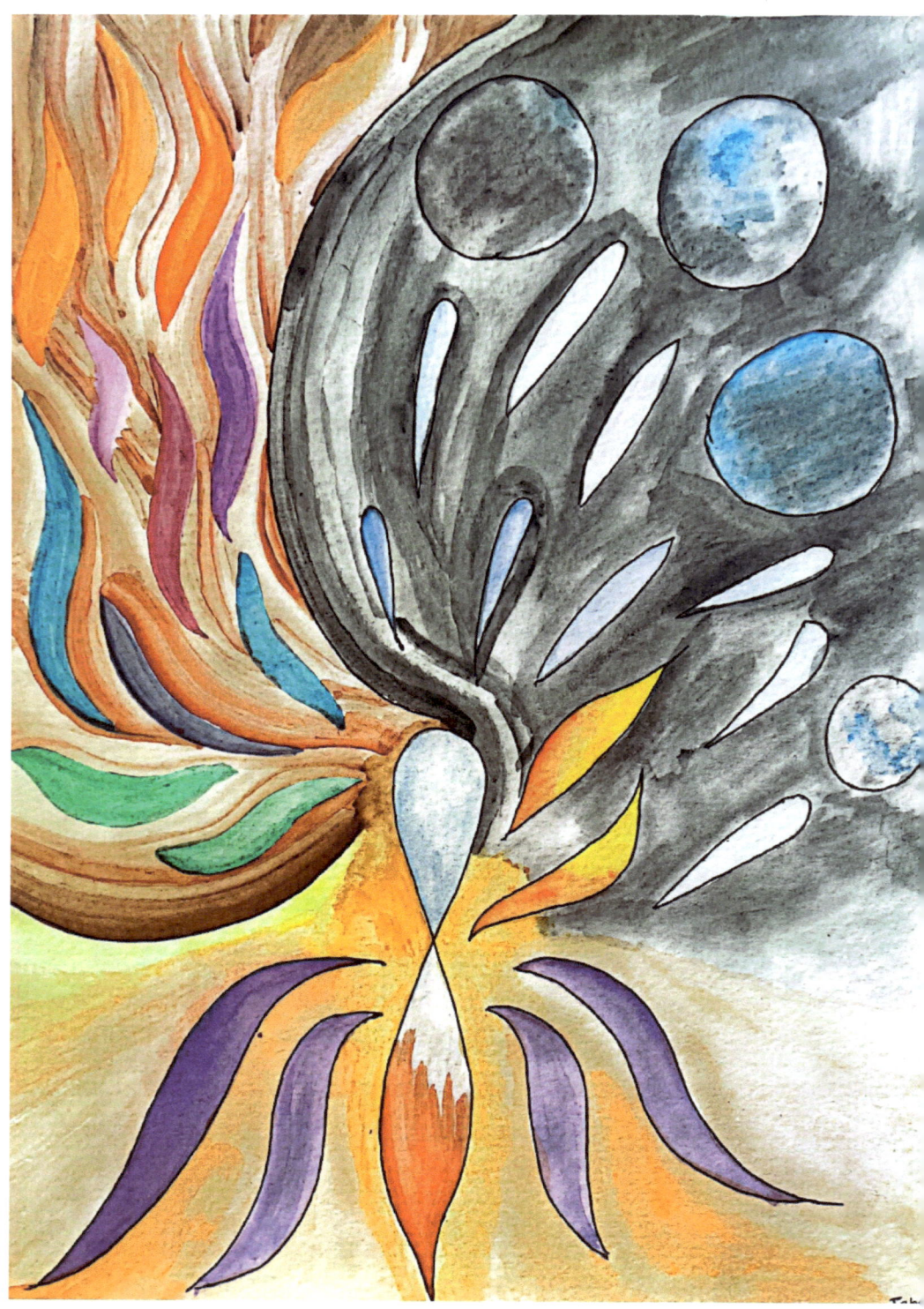

Duality

Duality of threat
Or was it a promise?
Ancestors well-met
Others far from bliss.

Energy thrown
and thrown straight back
The balance blown
for division's lack

Cold as ice
warm like fire
But wouldn't it be nice
let's not roast the ire

The question a-fear
Ban black and white
or colour by ear?
Both truths can be right.

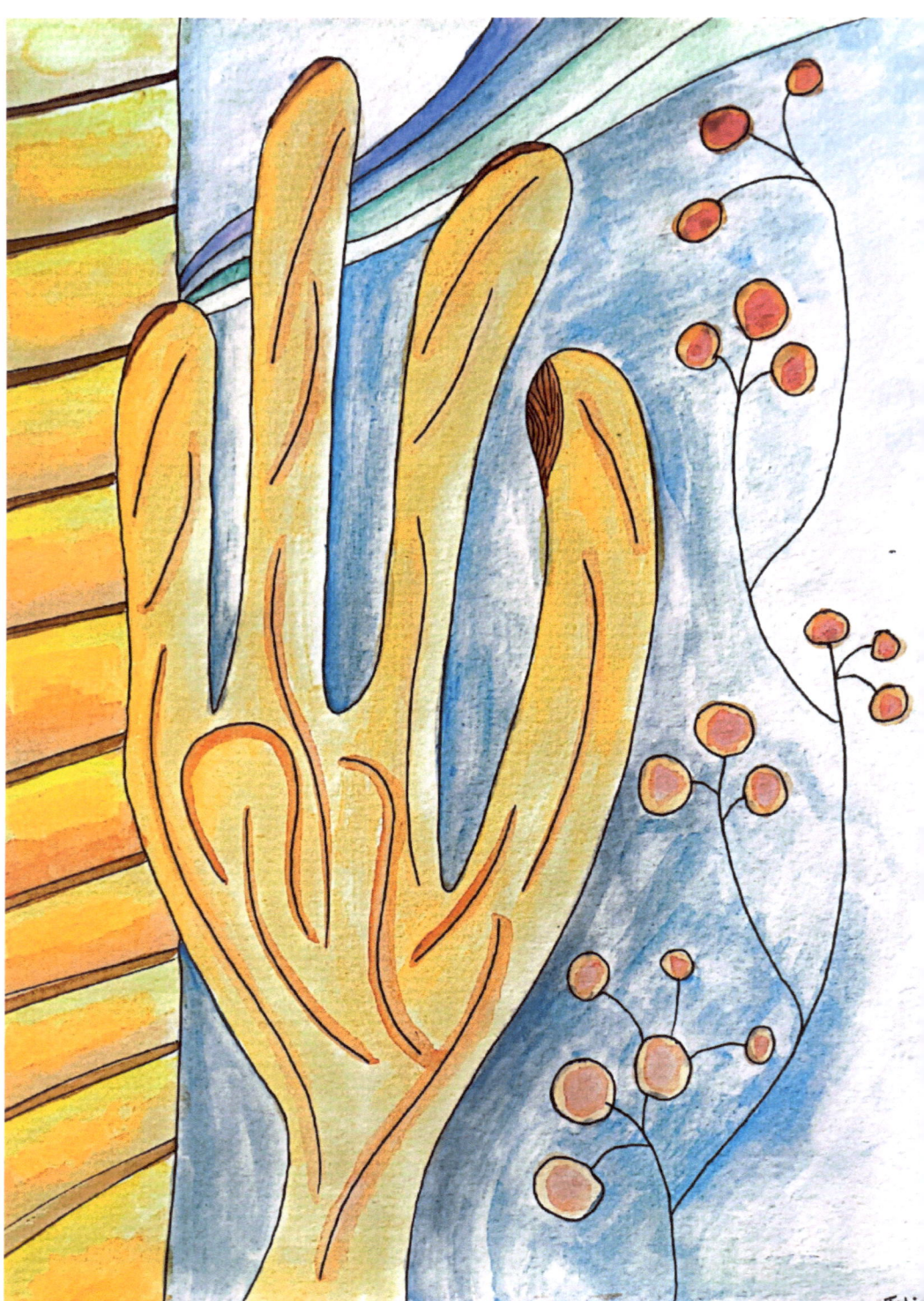

Perception

It's what it's always been
Look at your hand
Tell me what you have seen

Was is young, was it old?
Let me show you,
Time for time to hold.

Look, youth shines through
Then once again to age
the wisdom – this is how I do.

It's all perspective
So never mind the noise
for to know is to live

To live is a gift
And a hand can be both,
so why not let your eyes lift?

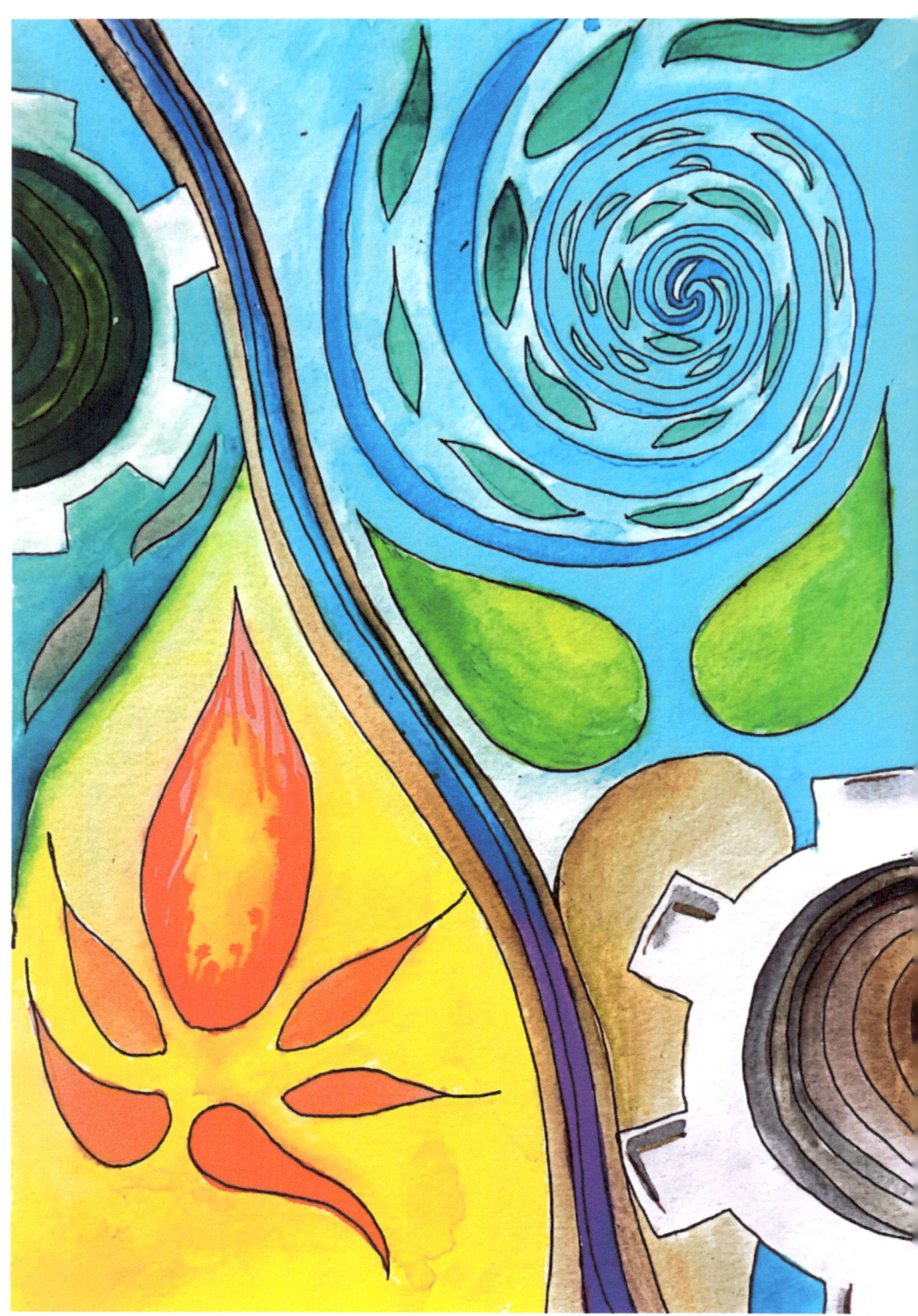

Cogs of the Universe

Letting your eyes lift
to the workings
of the universe is less
an escape than a moment -
of realisation

In duty and care
thought and action
morals and codes
there is room for radical honesty

Why reinvent the wheel
simply create ones own
and decorate it unique
sparkle forth and shine

www.ingramcontent.com/pod-product-compliance
Lightning Source LLC
Chambersburg PA
CBHW040306220526
45473CB00002B/598